WAYS
OF
DRAWING
THE HUMAN
Figure

**DAY AFTER DAY,
NEVER FAIL TO DRAW SOMETHING
WHICH, HOWEVER LITTLE IT MAY BE,
WILL YET IN THE END BE MUCH,
AND DO THY BEST.**

CENNINO CENNINI c.1390

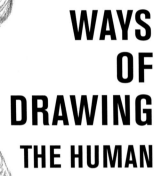

WAYS
OF
DRAWING
THE HUMAN

Figure

RUNNING PRESS
PHILADELPHIA • LONDON

**Produced, edited, and designed by Inklink,
Greenwich, London, England.**

Canadian representatives: General Publishing Co., Ltd.,
30 Lesmill Road, Don Mills, Ontario M3B 2T6.

9 8 7 6 5 4 3 2 1
Digit on the right indicates the number of this printing.

**WAYS OF DRAWING
THE HUMAN FIGURE,**
a guide to expanding
your visual awareness

Copyright © 1995 by Inklink

**This edition first published
in the United States by
Running Press Book
Publishers.**

Library of Congress
Catalog Number
94-67778

ISBN 1-56138-539-5

**CONSULTANT ARTISTS AND EDITORIAL BOARD
Concept and general editor, Simon Jennings
Contributing artist, Valerie Wiffen
Art-education adviser, Carolynn Cooke
Design and art direction, Simon Jennings
Text editors, Ian Kearey and Albert Jackson
Historical research, Ella Jennings and Peter Anderson**

Typeset in Akzidenz Grotesque, Bodoni, and Univers by Inklink
Printed by South Sea International Press, Hong Kong

This book may be ordered by mail from the publisher.
Please add $2.50 for postage and handling.
But try your bookstore first!

**Running Press Book Publishers
125 South Twenty-second Street
Philadelphia, Pennsylvania 19103-4399**

CONTENTS

Self-portrait
Charcoal pencil with white chalk on gray Ingres paper. Notice how the color and texture of the paper contribute to the quality and mood of the artist's drawing.

We are drawn to look at others of our kind from our first hour of life. The infinite variety of humanity is a vast resource for the artist, who stands in a place of special privilege, because drawing and painting are legitimate reasons for looking closely at people. Without observation and the gathering of genuine evidence, a drafter will only be able to produce generalities from memory, and these are often slick and unconvincing.

Only by looking with the naked eye can you select the necessary composition, emphasis, and information to make your drawings a plausible rendering of what you've seen. For the beginner, there is also a mental barrier to break around figure drawing, since there may be inhibitions about staring hard at other people, and anxieties about our ability to catch a tolerable likeness that will not offend another human being. Furthermore, that other person is quite likely to move frequently, if not all the time, unless they are a professional model!

The answers to these difficulties consist, first, in accepting that artists are held in affection and esteem by society, and that the task of recording what is seen and sharing that vision with others is a respected one. Next, realize that others may experience disappointment in relation to their expectations, but will not expect a professional result if it is understood that you are at the start of your artistic career. Finally, don't be too hard on your results — acknowledge successes when they come.

ANATOMY

Artistic awareness of anatomical knowledge relates to understanding and depicting the three-dimensional form of the body from what lies beneath the skin. The basic shape of the body is based on the vertically symmetrical pattern of the skeleton. This internal scaffolding is intricately jointed to enable the body to move freely, and it is important to remember that the framework of the living, moving body never holds the limp poses of the cadavers that are studied by medical students.

The surface figure that we draw is dictated by the muscular structure that covers the majority of the skeleton. Muscles control our every movement, in direct response to nervous messages sent along them from the brain.

Any variations in external body shape,

however small or large, will always relate directly to the basic bone-and-muscle structure. However, as with all visual work, you should observe each individual subject closely, because bodily proportions and dimensions vary from person to person, even before considerations of age and gender are taken into account.

The best way to put anatomical knowledge to practical, artistic use is to attend a life-drawing class or session, where you can observe how poses are created and made possible by different muscles and bones. Drawing from life is examined in detail later in this book, but a basic understanding of anatomy will make even the roughest sketches and studies more accurate and true to observation.

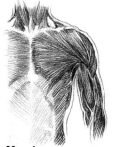

Muscles
Front view of the muscles of the neck, torso, and upper arm.

Bones
Foreshortened view of a ribcage and vertebrae.

The bones form the internal scaffolding of the human body. This drawing shows how the skeleton fits inside the overlying muscles and soft tissues, as well as identifying the important bones that make up the body shape and the contours of, here, an adult female.

Principal bones of the upper body

1	Cranium (skull)
2	Vertebrae (spine)
3	Clavicle (collarbone)
4	Scapula (shoulder blade)
5	Sternum (breastbone)
6	Rib cage

Principal bones of the limbs and lower body

7	Humerus
8	Radius
9	Ulna
10	Iliac fossa (hipbone)
11	Sacrum and coccyx
12	Femur (thighbone)
13	Patella (kneecap)
14	Tibia
15	Fibula

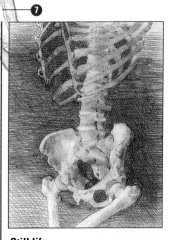

Still life

Most life-drawing classes have access to a human skeleton. Drawing this will help your understanding of the shape, form, and proportion of the human figure.

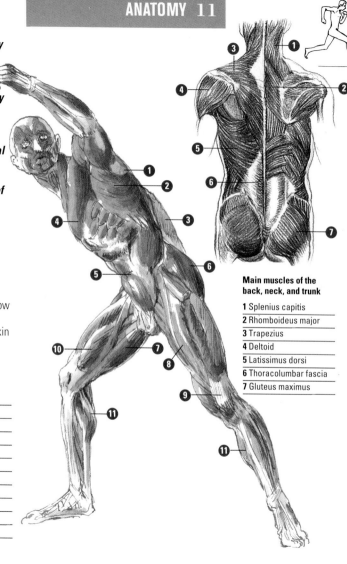

The musculature of the human body forms the upholstery or padding, and varies enormously from person to person. Some muscles change shape a great deal when put to use, and the amount and distribution of fatty tissue also determine the shape of each individual body.

Main muscles of the human body

These drawings show where the muscles appear under the skin and how they influence form.

1 Infraspinatus
2 Latissimus dorsi
3 Flexor carpi ulnaris
4 Pectoralis major
5 Rectus abdominis
6 Gluteus maximus
7 Gracilis
8 Rectus femoris
9 Tendon
10 Vastus medialis
11 Gastrocnemius

Main muscles of the back, neck, and trunk

1 Splenius capitis
2 Rhomboideus major
3 Trapezius
4 Deltoid
5 Latissimus dorsi
6 Thoracolumbar fascia
7 Gluteus maximus

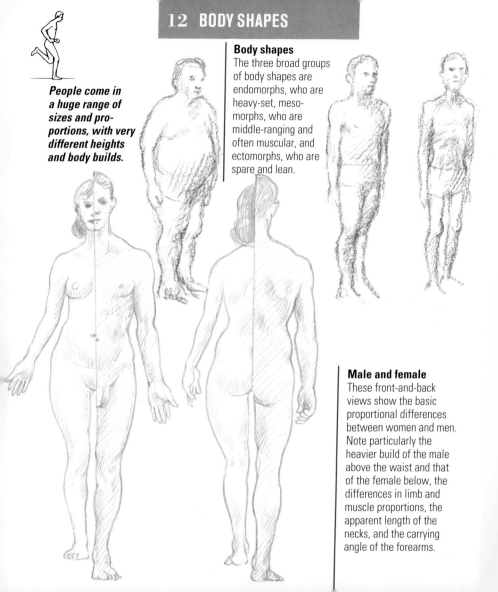

People come in a huge range of sizes and proportions, with very different heights and body builds.

Body shapes
The three broad groups of body shapes are endomorphs, who are heavy-set, meso-morphs, who are middle-ranging and often muscular, and ectomorphs, who are spare and lean.

Male and female
These front-and-back views show the basic proportional differences between women and men. Note particularly the heavier build of the male above the waist and that of the female below, the differences in limb and muscle proportions, the apparent length of the necks, and the carrying angle of the forearms.

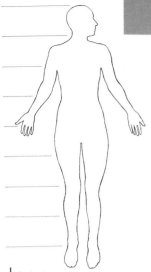

Relative proportions
The adult body can generally be divided up into eight head lengths, plus the distance from the middle of the ankle to the sole of the foot. The span of one's outstretched arms is roughly equal to one's height.

Moving shapes around
Artists sometimes manipulate proportions, for style, emotional effect, and to provoke different responses (right). You can experience something of this effect by catching reflections in concave or convex mirrors, which challenge a drafter by demanding thorough observation to capture unusual proportions.

Manipulating proportions
This bizarre effect was achieved by the artist drawing her reflection as seen in the curved surface of a shiny saucepan.

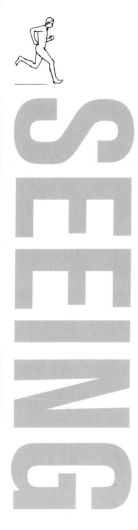

SEEING

To produce effective drawings of people, it is vital to look as much as possible at the real, live thing. "Secondhand" material, such as photographs, may be helpful on occasions, particularly for information about surfaces and textures, but won't produce great results if used as a sole source of inspiration.

Another important factor is to make an accumulative experience of hard observation that is focused on your subject; endeavor to make a mental record of the crucial facts, so that you train your visual memory. This will help to liberate you from preconceptions, which are usually misconceptions — especially if they are based on half-forgotten glances that registered little of what was happening visually. Sketches and visual notes will strengthen your drawing abilities, because you are learning to respond to a wide range of visual matter with representative marks.

The kind of observation required for drawing is the kind of hard look you give when driving before you pull out of a side road, to make sure that no other vehicle is approaching. If you pull out without looking, you could be hit by a truck. If you draw without looking, you may have accidents, too!

To give just one example, a vital aspect of observing the human figure is being aware of the constant adjustments that everyone must make to keep upright and stable. These involve minute changes to every part of the figure, and can only be drawn successfully when you have looked with purpose.

Observation
Learning to look hard helps you find inspiration in every-day scenes.

Background
Detail from *De Humani Corporis Fabrica*, by Andreas Vesalius (1514–64)

Every mark you make should represent something you see. This is easier to achieve in a life-drawing session or with a model than when trying to capture moving figures, where accuracy is relative, and the criteria are necessarily different. But it's better to have just a few well-observed lines on each page than dozens of badly observed marks and drawings.

Over and over

It is impossible to make too many drawings, particularly when you are starting as an artist. Drawing the same subjects over and over can be helpful, so long as you determine to learn from each effort.

Correcting errors

Contrary to some theories, if you've made a mark you are entitled to erase it. The important thing is not to delete the mistake until you have made a better mark; it is not uncommon to see inexperienced artists erase a wrong line and then draw exactly the same line again. Keep the error and use it as a starting point for a correction, and ensure that the new line is satisfactory before erasing the mistake.

Changing your mind

If something looks wrong, or if you change your mind about part of a drawing, change the mark the moment you notice the problem. If you don't, the error becomes part of the composition, and affects all other marks on the paper.

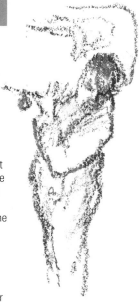

The value of quick work

Very quick sketches, when you don't have the opportunity to make finished drawings (far right and left), are useful for building up a library of work to refer to later. These used oil pastel.

Overcoming difficulties

Sometimes figure drawing may seem difficult. In this case, concentrate on the overall effect, and try to relax while drawing; the difficulties may not be so great once you are warmed up. Ambition is not a bad thing, but it's wise to temper your expectations. Each drawing session should be taken as it comes. Learn to pace yourself and to find ways to get the best drawing possible out of every situation.

Evaluating your work

Learn to evaluate your drawings after a period of time, so you can look clearly and dispassionately at your work. When a drawing is finished, put it away and leave it for perhaps several months before coming back to it. Never throw anything away immediately – you need disasters to learn from, as well as successes and triumphs!

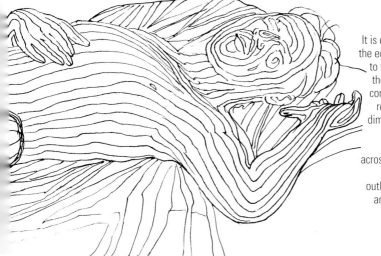

Contours

It is easy to focus on the edges of a figure, to the detriment of the form. Drawing contours helps you realize the three-dimensional nature of the body and makes you look across the form. This drawing was outlined in charcoal and then inked in.

Seen diagramm-atically, the body is a symmetrical structure, with pairs of arms, legs, feet, hands, eyes, and ears appearing the same on both sides. This is not the case in reality, where the artist has to deal with pose and perspective.

Balance
These sketches demonstrate how we keep our balance by constantly making adjustments between the upper body (thorax) and hips. Look out for this when drawing.

Weight distribution
The standing figure, drawn in graphite pencil, shows that the weight of the body is normally taken by one side or the other.

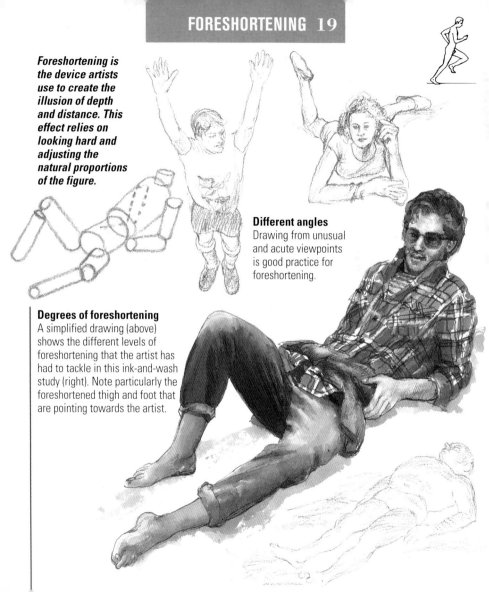

Foreshortening is the device artists use to create the illusion of depth and distance. This effect relies on looking hard and adjusting the natural proportions of the figure.

Different angles
Drawing from unusual and acute viewpoints is good practice for foreshortening.

Degrees of foreshortening
A simplified drawing (above) shows the different levels of foreshortening that the artist has had to tackle in this ink-and-wash study (right). Note particularly the foreshortened thigh and foot that are pointing towards the artist.

Charcoal pencil (left); charcoal stick, heightened with charcoal pencil and wash (main image)

Because many subjects will be on the move, you will have to work quickly and cultivate your memory to get what you've seen down on paper. Try some of the techniques shown here to capture your subject ; use broad strokes and washes to represent the totality of the vision, and also try capturing the essence of a situation with an accurate, yet economical, line.

Studies of sporting events employing broad-stroke and wash techniques to record moving figures

Shading, blocking, and washes
While it is possible to make drawings
using only lines, this can be uphill work
for the beginner: linear marks are
essentially two-dimensional, and it is
difficult to make them represent a three-
dimensional subject. Shading, blocking
in with color or tone, and watercolor
washes are good ways to suggest the
solidity of a figure.

**Pastel pencil with a
watercolor wash and
gray-ink wash
for the shadows**

**These little
running figures
are drawn in
brush and wash**

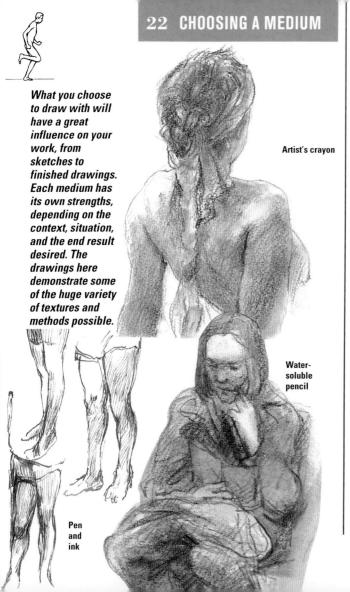

What you choose to draw with will have a great influence on your work, from sketches to finished drawings. Each medium has its own strengths, depending on the context, situation, and the end result desired. The drawings here demonstrate some of the huge variety of textures and methods possible.

Artist's crayon

Water-soluble pencil

Pen and ink

Artist's crayon

These suit artists used to drawing with pencils; they can also be used for filling in tone and are easy to erase or soften, using a paper stump.

Water-soluble pencils

Also known as watercolor or aquarelle pencils. Used in the same way as regular pencils, but they can be wetted to make a watercolor-like wash. Carry a small, dampened, sponge to soften lines and make fluid washes.

Pen and ink

You need to use pen and ink with confidence, because it is difficult to erase marks once they are made – note the corrected lines in these sketches of legs. However, pen and ink is an expressive medium, capable of fine detail and subtle, defining shades.

Litho pencil with brown-and-gray wash

Combining media widens your choice of textures and colors, and it's worth discovering which media work best together. Don't be afraid to experiment with materials.

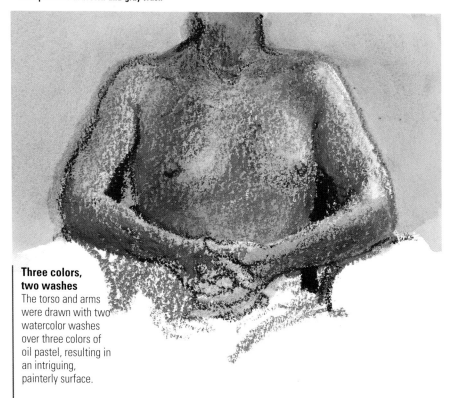

Three colors, two washes
The torso and arms were drawn with two watercolor washes over three colors of oil pastel, resulting in an intriguing, painterly surface.

These sketches use watercolor pencils to create shading and wash effects

Making sketches in the studio and in everyday situations will improve your visual memory and sharpen your powers of observation. Because you do not have the luxury of spending much time on a single figure or pose, your drawing speed should improve, and the more you sketch, the better your eye-to-hand coordination will become. Keeping a sketchbook will provide you with a large visual library of images and act as a pictorial diary.

Sketching on journeys

These drawings were created on one journey on the subway; the artist used graphite and water-soluble pencils to capture the poses of her fellow passengers. To avoid drawing attention to yourself in public places, make your sketches in a small sketchbook.

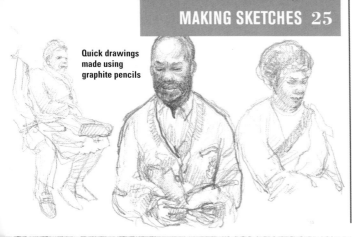

Quick drawings made using graphite pencils

Visual notes
This sketch (below) incorporates color notes for working out a finished drawing. The musicians were drawn during their performance in a concert hall; soft charcoal and a paper stump were used.

Drawing heads is a subject in its own right. Facial expressions and emotions can be portrayed through simple lines in a quick sketch, or worked up in a more highly finished drawing.

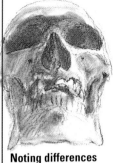

Noting differences
Not all heads are the same shape: there are long and short skulls, rounded and elongated heads, and different features, all of which are there to observe and record (above and top left).

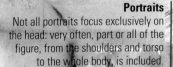

Using your time
These studies of heads were made during a life-drawing session, when the artist was concentrating on one part of the figure for a while.

Portraits
Not all portraits focus exclusively on the head: very often, part or all of the figure, from the shoulders and torso to the whole body, is included.

Attention to detail
Learn how to draw individual features convincingly – ears and hair, for example. These details, correctly observed, will lend realism and likeness to your heads.

Space and lighting
The head dominates the foreground of this composition drawn in charcoal pencil. The erect forearm frames the face, and the figure is placed in an intimate space suggested by the objects on the bureau. Light from the lamp creates strong shadows throughout the composition and highlights that define the profile of the face.

Arms are tremendously expressive limbs – think of how dancers use them, and how much body language resides in arms, hands, and shoulders.

Media

Arms are a good subject for trying out similar, "pointed" media, such as graphite pencils, charcoal pencils, and artist's crayons. Vary your technique, and experiment with alternative textures.

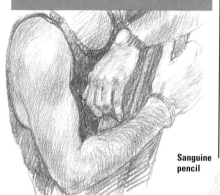

Sanguine pencil

Charcoal pencil

6B (very soft) pencil

2B (soft) pencil

Flexibility

Arms and hands are able to take more positions than any other part of the body. The contrast with the less-supple torso can be used to add variety to your drawings. When setting up a pose or observing a subject, keep looking for angles that add interest and tension to your composition.

Artist's crayon

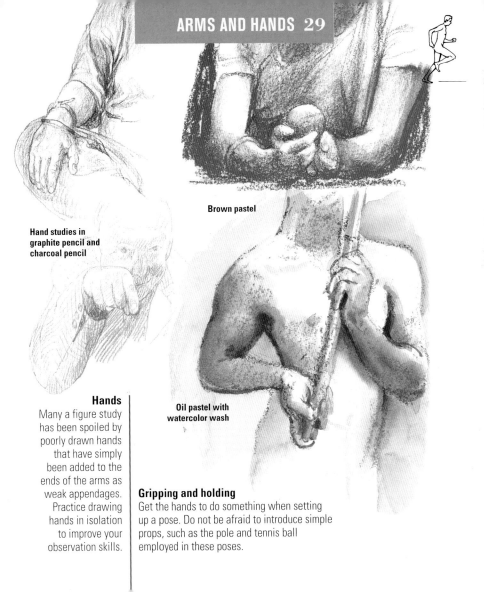

Brown pastel

**Hand studies in
graphite pencil and
charcoal pencil**

**Oil pastel with
watercolor wash**

Hands

Many a figure study
has been spoiled by
poorly drawn hands
that have simply
been added to the
ends of the arms as
weak appendages.
Practice drawing
hands in isolation
to improve your
observation skills.

Gripping and holding

Get the hands to do something when setting
up a pose. Do not be afraid to introduce simple
props, such as the pole and tennis ball
employed in these poses.

It may help to think of legs as essentially columnar in structure, with surface variations. Their range of poses is similar to those made by a jointed tube – but not as simple – with a reasonably limited number of possible angles of movement.

Shape

The thickness of the thigh is due to the massive vastus lateralis muscles, while the patella creates the distinctive knee shape. The curve of the calves is the soleus muscle tapering to the protruding maleolus (ankle bone).

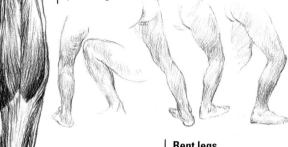

Bent legs

The same pose will look very different from the front, sides, and back of the legs; pay particular attention to where the highlights occur from changing viewpoints.

Foreshortening

This can be daunting; one way of making it easier is to hold your drawing instrument up to the level of the leg you are observing and tilt it to the angle of the limb. This will give you an idea of the spatial relation-ships when you are drawing the legs.

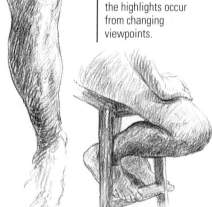

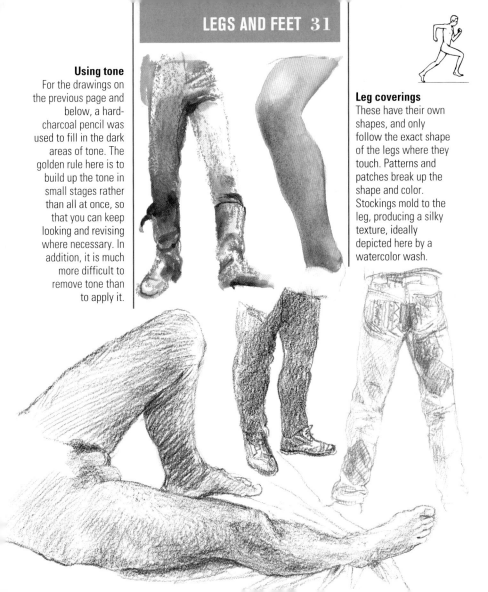

Using tone
For the drawings on the previous page and below, a hard-charcoal pencil was used to fill in the dark areas of tone. The golden rule here is to build up the tone in small stages rather than all at once, so that you can keep looking and revising where necessary. In addition, it is much more difficult to remove tone than to apply it.

Leg coverings
These have their own shapes, and only follow the exact shape of the legs where they touch. Patterns and patches break up the shape and color. Stockings mold to the leg, producing a silky texture, ideally depicted here by a watercolor wash.

Since the Renaissance, drawing and painting the naked human form have been the backbone of serious art study. To make a life-drawing session run smoothly, it is best to use professional models; they can probably be contacted through a local art group, which will collectively hire the model. Many adult-education centers run life-drawing classes, and drawing in groups is a good way to meet other artists, to compare and discuss work.

Working with your model

You will probably get better results if the model can play a creative part in the session; he or she should be consulted about poses, or you can allow him or her to choose those that are the most comfortable for long periods. (All the life-drawing poses in this book were chosen by the models, in consultation with the artist.) About an hour for each pose is standard, but be advised by the model if you are not sure. Regular breaks are essential, and the model should be allowed to relax and keep warm between poses. Don't forget to provide somewhere for the model to change.

Location and environment

Try to arrange the session in a reasonably large, warm space, so that the artists are able to set up and draw from whatever angle they choose; it's difficult to produce satisfactory work when you haven't chosen the viewpoint or are unhappy with it.

Clothing and props

Decide collectively beforehand whether you wish to use drapery, props, or clothing in the session, and how it is to be provided; if you ask, the model may be able to bring items.

Wide-ranging possibilities

A life-drawing session can expand your artistic boundaries. Your viewpoint, your chosen medium, the model's pose, the lighting and background – all these will have a material effect on how your drawings will turn out.

Look before you leap

Don't be afraid to move around the life room looking for the viewpoint that suits you most and allows you to settle in for a long session. If need be, make preliminary sketches; if you're still not happy, try another viewpoint.

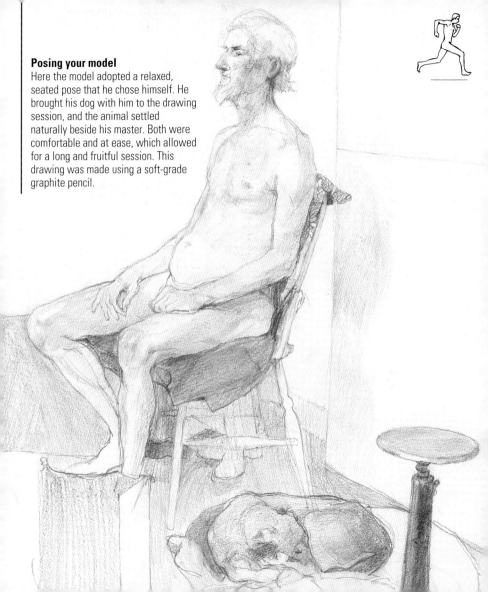

Posing your model

Here the model adopted a relaxed, seated pose that he chose himself. He brought his dog with him to the drawing session, and the animal settled naturally beside his master. Both were comfortable and at ease, which allowed for a long and fruitful session. This drawing was made using a soft-grade graphite pencil.

Framing and composition

Consider how the model will best be placed on your paper, and where the edge will cut off the image. In general, it's sensible not to have heads or feet disappearing out of the bottom or top of the work, but artists sometimes do this for a particular effect, as in the sketch below.

Background

When drawing from life, it is worth paying attention to the background, whether or not you include it in your drawing. The light reflected from dark and pale walls is different, and this will affect the way you see line and form. In this drawing (right) the dark background gives depth to the composition and provides a dynamic contrast to the model's flesh tone, which has been worked back from an overall, dark-graphite surface with an eraser.

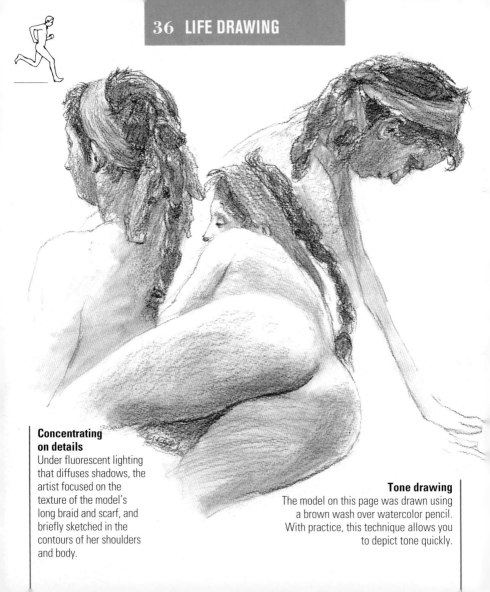

Concentrating on details
Under fluorescent lighting that diffuses shadows, the artist focused on the texture of the model's long braid and scarf, and briefly sketched in the contours of her shoulders and body.

Tone drawing
The model on this page was drawn using a brown wash over watercolor pencil. With practice, this technique allows you to depict tone quickly.

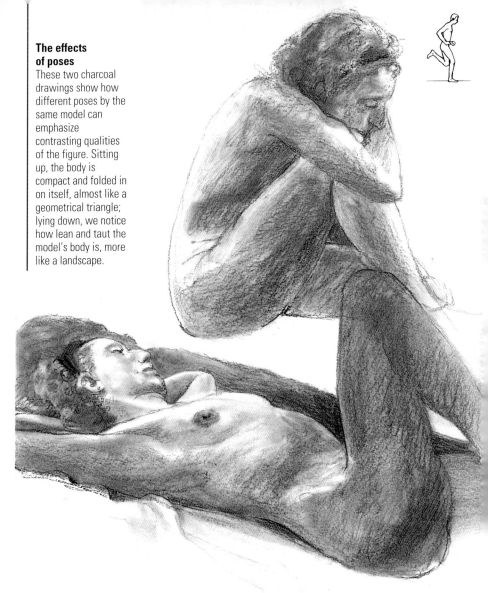

The effects of poses

These two charcoal drawings show how different poses by the same model can emphasize contrasting qualities of the figure. Sitting up, the body is compact and folded in on itself, almost like a geometrical triangle; lying down, we notice how lean and taut the model's body is, more like a landscape.

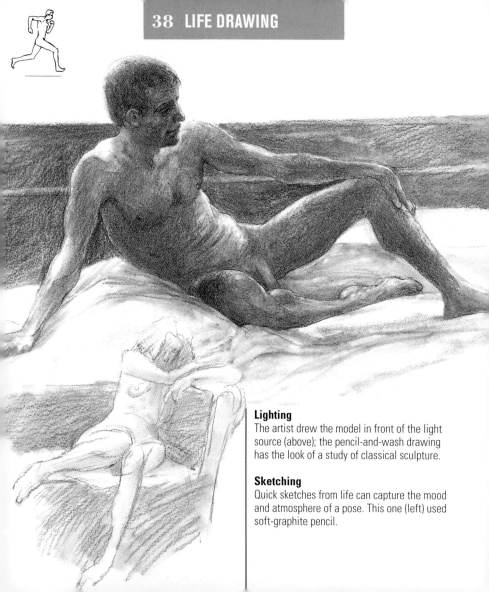

Lighting
The artist drew the model in front of the light source (above); the pencil-and-wash drawing has the look of a study of classical sculpture.

Sketching
Quick sketches from life can capture the mood and atmosphere of a pose. This one (left) used soft-graphite pencil.

Viewpoints

Choosing a viewpoint starts from the moment you take your stance or sit down. It has a crucial influence on your end results, as it will dictate exactly how much, from what angle, and which scale you see. Pastel-pencil drawing (right).

Five-minute studies

You don't always have to spend the entire time drawing the whole figure in a life-drawing session – concentrate on whatever limb or detail you feel is important or needs more practice (left).

The majority of figures you draw will be clothed or, at least, draped, and in a normal situation will be engaged in some kind of activity that will include props, such as a shovel for digging the road, or a shopping bag or basket.

Variety and contrast
When you are sketching, people will inevitably be doing something as they go about their everyday lives. This provides a great opportunity to include props and costumes in your drawings, as shown in this lively sketch-book page.

Telltale clothing
Clothing can immediately establish a social identity, enhance or disguise the figure inside, or be cut, patterned, or colored in ways the human body cannot. Clothes tell us something about the occupation and character of the figure, and can inform us about the weather and climate of the location or setting.

Apart from a hired model, no one else will want to keep still for you for very long, and in many cases your subjects will be on the move anyway. This means getting motion and action into your drawings. It may be tempting to use photographs, but they will not give you the most accurate results and should be used with caution.

Go where the action is

The artist spent an afternoon drawing people in a swimming pool, using a water-soluble pencil, wetted with a small brush for washes. As well as capturing the movement of the bodies, she was looking to depict the distorting quality of the water.

Composites
If you can't finish a complete figure, try making composites. Eventually you will have a plausible and informative drawing, and while it may be like no one particular person, it will have the veracity of observed work, unlike copying photographs.

A quick medium
If the movement that you wish to catch is unlikely to be repeated, use a fast medium – here, oil pastel – to achieve the most complete end results.

As always, the most important point when drawing children is direct and accurate observation. Don't assume that they are adults in miniature, because this produces unconvincing results. Spend time watching children and get to know their unique proportions and characteristics.

Proportions

On average, the body length of a newborn baby is equal to about four head lengths, at age six it's about six head lengths, and at age twelve it's roughly seven head lengths.

Heads

The shape of the head and the relationship between the facial features demand special attention. Hatching the contours of the face with a graphite pencil is an effective way to quickly depict smooth skin; the same medium was used for all the drawings on this page.

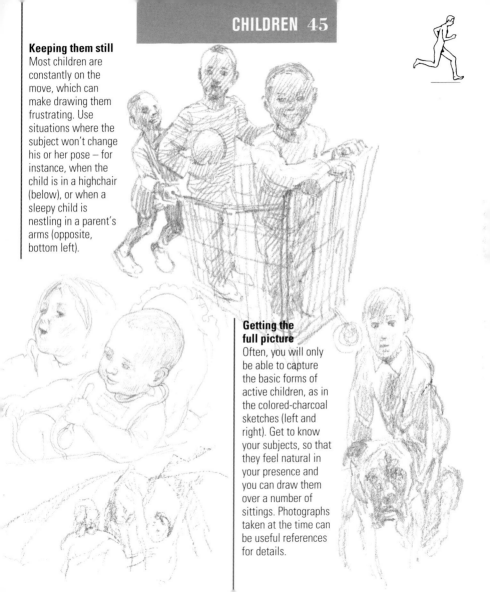

Keeping them still
Most children are constantly on the move, which can make drawing them frustrating. Use situations where the subject won't change his or her pose – for instance, when the child is in a highchair (below), or when a sleepy child is nestling in a parent's arms (opposite, bottom left).

Getting the full picture
Often, you will only be able to capture the basic forms of active children, as in the colored-charcoal sketches (left and right). Get to know your subjects, so that they feel natural in your presence and you can draw them over a number of sittings. Photographs taken at the time can be useful references for details.

Drawing more than one figure allows you to express relationships and emotions, such as friendship, love, indifference, a common purpose, or a mass focus of attention, that are not possible with a single figure.

Quick sketches
There may not be enough time to add much detail when sketching groups or crowds, in which case a hat, scarf, or pair of eyeglasses suffice to portray individuality.

Illusion of mass
The actual mass of the crowd is a simple texture, a kind of shorthand for people. The more detailed figures in the foreground make the scene true-to-life and convincing.

Building up a crowd
This group of people was not drawn as a unit, but was built up from the same viewpoint at a market. The artist used a broad lithographic pencil; this must be used confidently, because it is hard to erase; however, it is versatile and doesn't smear. It is also possible to assemble your own crowd scene from individual studies made at different times in your sketchbook.

Choice of medium

Crowds and groups can be effectively portrayed in detail by using a linear medium, such as graphite or charcoal pencil, or pen and ink, or as a mass of tone and color, using charcoal, watercolor washes, or pastels, for example. Combine the two types of medium to produce rich, colorful studies.

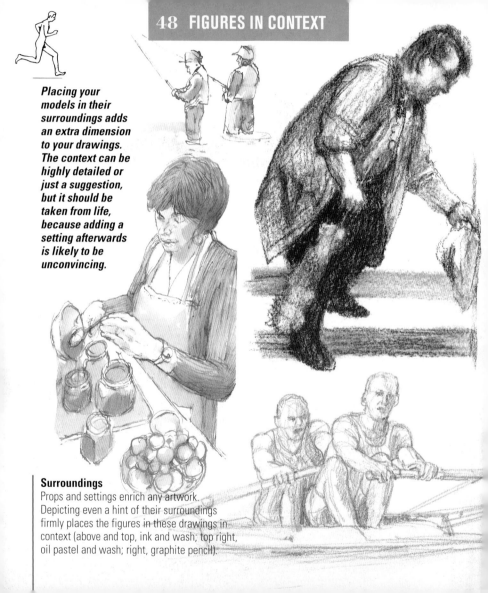

Placing your models in their surroundings adds an extra dimension to your drawings. The context can be highly detailed or just a suggestion, but it should be taken from life, because adding a setting afterwards is likely to be unconvincing.

Surroundings

Props and settings enrich any artwork. Depicting even a hint of their surroundings firmly places the figures in these drawings in context (above and top, ink and wash; top right, oil pastel and wash; right, graphite pencil).

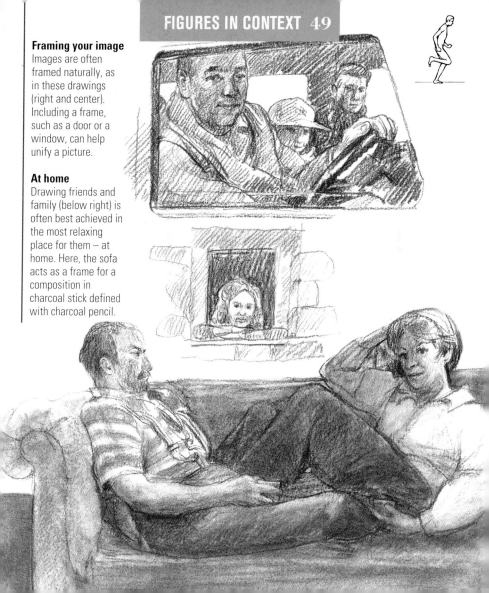

Framing your image
Images are often framed naturally, as in these drawings (right and center). Including a frame, such as a door or a window, can help unify a picture.

At home
Drawing friends and family (below right) is often best achieved in the most relaxing place for them – at home. Here, the sofa acts as a frame for a composition in charcoal stick defined with charcoal pencil.

To make a finished, concentrated figure study, you will need the cooperation of a patient model; failing this, draw a self-portrait.

A patient model
A sick friend was happy to model for the artist, wearing a nightgown and sitting propped up in bed. The white highlights of the clothing were emphasized by dramatic lighting from a table lamp, and became the focus of the drawing.

Self-portrait
In this self-portrait of the author (see also page 6), the mirror is on the other side of the doorframe from the artist; this creates a sense of depth and space, and makes a frame within a frame.

Setting up a self-portrait
The majority of full-length self-portraits show the artist at an easel or drawing board. You will need a reasonably large mirror for full-length self-portraits; if working from a wall-mounted mirror, arrange mobile mirrors to capture different angles.

Photographs make acceptable artist's reference material, provided you use them as you would use sketches, and not as an end in themselves. A good photograph is a creative two-dimensional image in its own right, and a straight copy is not going to bring anything to it: in fact, the photograph will probably be better.

When to use photographs

Photographs are especially useful in situations when there is very little time for drawing – such as when working with an active child, for example. Always try to make a few sketches at the same time, to augment your photographic record, and take as many shots as possible from different viewpoints during the session. The sketches will tell you something about the three-dimensional nature of the living person, while the photographs will capture the things you may not be able to include in quick sketches, such as textures and small details.

The importance of the sketchbook
Some artists build a library of sketchbooks with notes and part drawings, as well as photographs and pictures cut from newspapers and magazines. These can be used as supplementary information to add to unfinished drawings made on the spot.

Beware of distortion

When taking your own reference photographs, don't forget that camera lenses distort, particularly wide-angle lenses. This is the type of lens often used in instant and automatic cameras, and your drawings will need to be adjusted accordingly.

Building a reference library

If you are interested in particular themes for your drawings, it pays to build a reference library, comprising your own photographs, with cuttings from newspapers and magazines, so that you will have a rich variety of viewpoints, lighting conditions, and people to draw upon.

Lay figures
You may find it useful to use a wooden lay figure, or mannequin, as sold in art-supply stores, to help work out a pose where people's actions were too fast for you to capture the whole of what you saw.

BASIC ESSENTIALS

The only essential equipment you need for drawing is a pencil and a piece of paper. But, as your experience grows and your skills develop, you will hopefully discover your own drawing style. As this happens, you will probably develop a preference for using particular art materials. Throughout this book you will have seen references to a variety of art terms, materials, and techniques, some of which may be new to you. The following is a glossary of useful information that relates to the artwork featured in this book.

MATERIALS

Graphite pencil
The common, "lead" pencil, available in a many qualities and price ranges. The graphite core (lead) is graded from softness to hardness: 9B is very, very soft, and 9H is very, very hard. HB is the middle grade. For drawing work, start around 2B.

Colored pencil
A generic term for all pencils with a colored core. There is an enormous variety of colors and qualities available. They also vary in softness and hardness, but this is seldom indicated on the packet.

Litho pencil
A greasy pencil that glides quickly over paper and reacts well with rough textures.

Water-soluble pencil
Capable of creating a variety of effects, by either wetting the tip of the pencil or using dampened paper.

Charcoal
Charcoal drawing sticks, made from charred willow or vine twigs, are available in three grades: soft, medium, and hard. Soft charcoal is ideal for blending and smudging; the harder varieties are better for linear drawing. In pencil form, charcoal is cleaner and more controllable.

Artist's crayons
Square drawing sticks in traditional, "earth" colors, such as sanguine, bistre, red, and sepia.

Pastels
Soft drawing sticks made by blending colored pigments with chalk or clay, bound with gum. Oil pastels, made using an animal-fat binder, are less crumbly. Both types are available in a very wide range of colors and tones, as are pastel pencils.

Drawing ink
There is a variety of inks available, from water-soluble, writing (fountain pen or calligraphy) inks to thick, permanent, and waterproof drawing inks. India ink is a traditional drawing ink: it is waterproof and very dense, drying with an interesting, shiny surface. The inks are available in many colors, and can be thinned down with distilled water for creating washes.

Steel-nib (dip) pen
The old-fashioned, dip-in-the-inkwell pen; a worthy and versatile drawing instrument. You may want to experiment with nibs for thickness and flexibility, but just a single nib can make a variety of line widths as you alter the pressure on the pen.

Paper
Varies enormously in type, quality, texture, manufacture, and price. Paper is graded from smooth to rough, and is either smooth (hot-pressed, or HP), medium (cold-pressed, or CP), or rough. The smoothness or roughness of a paper is known as the "tooth." For example, the tooth of a watercolor paper is generally more marked, and rougher than that of a cartridge paper for drawing. The tooth of a paper will influence the way that a medium reacts to it.

Paper stump
Strip of paper twisted into a narrow cone. The point is used to blend and soften charcoal or pastel.

TERMS

Drybrush
A drawing effect created by using a sparsely-loaded brush, often with watercolor, or dry, fiber-tip pen. Drybrush allows the texture of the paper or any drawing beneath to show through.

Mixed media
Drawing using two or more materials.

Line drawing
A drawing made up purely of linear marks, with no attempt to indicate shadow or darker areas through shading or hatching.

Brush drawing
A drawing made solely with a brush.

Wash
The free application of a transparent color or tone to a drawing, usually by paintbrush.

Shading
Shadow or dark areas in a drawing, made by darkening the overall surface of the area.

Tone
The prevailing shade in a drawing, and its comparative dullness or brightness.

Blocking in
A generic term to describe any tone or texture not made purely by linear marks.

Highlights
The lighter points in a drawing. These are generally the points where light strikes an object, such as a reflection in an eye, or on a surface.

Hatching
An illusion of shadow, tone, or texture in a drawing, indicated by closely drawn lines.

Crosshatching
An illusion of darker shadows, tones, or textures, indicated by overlayering hatched lines at differing angles to each other.

Parallel hatching
Shadows, tones, or textures, indicated by drawing lines next to one another.

Dot and stipple
An illusion of darker shadows, tones, or textures, indicated by small dots, usually made with the pointed tip of the drawing instrument.

POSSIBILITIES

INDEX OF POSSIBILITIES There are many ways of looking at the world, and there are as many ways of interpreting it. Art and creativity in drawing are not just about "correctness" or only working in a narrow, prescribed manner; they are about the infinite ways of seeing a three-dimensional object and setting it down.

In the earlier sections of this book, the consultant artist demonstrated some of her different approaches to drawing a specific subject. Her examples show how she has developed a personal way of seeing and setting down human forms.

The following section of images is intended to further help you discover and develop your own creativity. It is an index of possibilities: an indication of just some of the inventive and inspirational directions that creative artists have taken and continue to take. This visual glossary demonstrates how the same subject can be treated in a variety of ways, and how different cultures and artistic conventions can affect treatments.

In every culture and age, symbols and simplified images are vital factors in communication. The earliest cave drawings reduce the forms of men and animals to the basics, and tell an immediate story; similarly, modern advertising campaigns and computer-based, corporate trademarks depend on our instant recognition of simplified forms. The graphic images in this section show how the artist's eye and hand can produce universally understood forms in all human societies.

A major part of artistic and technical development is being aware of, and open to, possibilities from outside your chosen sphere. To that end, the images in this section use a wide variety of materials and techniques. They may not all be pure "drawing," but each one expands the boundaries of what is possible, and provides new ways of seeing and interpreting figures.

Anthropomorphic Figure
Iran-India, 1000 BC
Cast bronze

Goddess Nut
Detail from a
sarcophagus
Egypt, *c.* 600 BC
Engraving

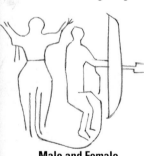

Male and Female Figures
Detail from
Paleolithic engraving
Africa, *c.* 1200 BC
Engraving on rock

Athlete Receiving a Medal
Detail from
a vase
Greece,
500-475 BC
Paint on
pottery

Dancing Girl
Brihadish-
varasvamin
(*fl.* 11th century)
India, *c.* 1000
Wall painting

Venus
Sandro Botticelli
(1445–1510)
Italy, 1482
Oil on panel

The Three Graces
Raphael
(Raffaelo Santi)
(1483–1520)
Italy, 1500
Oil on canvas

David
Michelangelo
Buonarroti
(1475–1564)
Italy, 1504
Marble

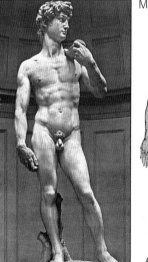

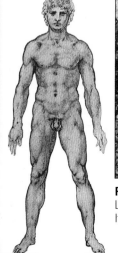

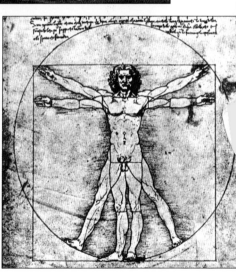

Proportional Studies (left and above)
Leonardo da Vinci (1452–1519)
Italy, c. 1500. Pen and ink

Oscar Wilde
Vanity Fair caricature
Carlo Pellegrini
(1839–89)
England, 1884
Watercolor

Seated Young Girl
Egon Schiele
(1890–1918)
Austria, 1910
Pencil and gouache

Lady Jane Grey
Attributed to Master
John (*fl.* 16th century)
England, *c.* 1545
Oil on panel

Woman Gleaning
Vincent van Gogh
(1853–90)
Holland, 1885
Chalk and wash

Les Demoiselles d'Avignon
Pablo Picasso
(1881–1973)
France, 1907
Oil on canvas

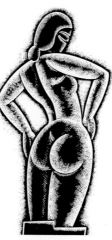

The Gravedigger
Kasimir Malevitch
(1878–1935)
Russia, 1913
Crayon and watercolor

The Child-stealers
Jean Cocteau
(1891–1963)
France, 1928
Pen and ink

Sculpture No. 2
Eric Gill
(1882–1940)
England, 1930
Woodcut

Nude
Raoul Dufy
(1877–1953)
France, 1936
Pen and ink

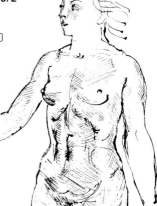

Icarus, the Circus
Henri Matisse (1869–1954)
France, 1947
Gouache and cut paper

Man in a Doorway
L. S. Lowry
(1887–1976)
England, 1964
Oil on canvas

Human Form
Joan Miró (1893–1983)
Spain, 1950
Lithograph

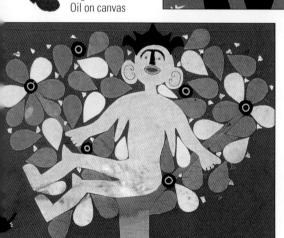

Female Guardian (Goddess)
Asafo (warrior) flag of the Fanté tribe
Ghana, c.1930
Appliqué and embroidery on cloth

Alice and José
Alice Neel (1900–84)
USA, 1938
Pastel

Untitled
David Austen
(b. 1960)
England, 1988
Pen and ink

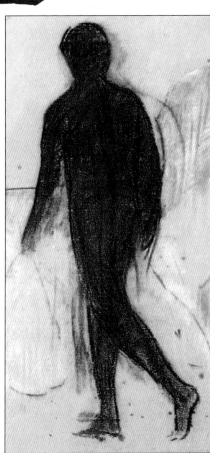

L'homme Primitif
Odilon Redon
(1840–1916)
France, c. 1915–16
Pastel

Nude Figures
Roger Hilton (1911–75)
England, 1972–5
Charcoal and pencil

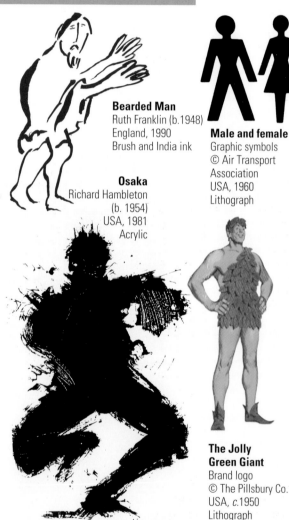

Bearded Man
Ruth Franklin (b.1948)
England, 1990
Brush and India ink

Male and female
Graphic symbols
© Air Transport
Association
USA, 1960
Lithograph

Osaka
Richard Hambleton
(b. 1954)
USA, 1981
Acrylic

```
                left hand
                how grows
                the outsided
                others others of
                doesnt show this
                ofthe other man
            the outside world not
                yes to the
                hand to
                others
                hand
                hand
                hand
                hand
                hand
                hand
                hand
                hand
                hand
                hand
                hand
                hand
        thumbs to do withr repressed out in i
    will power has taken a kick does not att
  inside fingertips missing certian part repres
    inside inside somthing else
    left hand is not as strong outt
    palm areas emotional support
    frustration streamers doesnot
    the outside world world nott
    certain missing repressed yes
    the the hte df jigut the the t
    will power will power will pow
    the the the the th ethe the the
    the the the the the the the th
    support supportinn outer
  geens are the the the the
    outer inner outer inn
    secure secure out
    then frustratio
        jer       y too
        out       out
        the       the
        inn       inn
        wre       wre
        sta       sta
        boo       boo
        rat       rat
        the       the
        uko       pko
        art       art
        mer       mer
        inn       nni
        tss       sst
        onn       onn
        inn       inn
        fru       fru
        out       out
        ere       ere
        fws       fws
        yyi       yyi
        qaz       qaz
        wsx       wsx
        edc       edc
        tgb       tgb
        asd       asd
        wer       wer
        ert       ert
        dc        dc
        uk        uk
        yo        yo
    therodynami   therrodynamiy
    somthingeise  somthingeise
    goodbyebye    goodbyebye
  certain part repres  repress part certain
  insideinsideinside   insideinsideinside
  traintickt trainticke trainticket trainticket
```

Text Man
Peter B. J. Anderson
(b. 1969)
England, 1992
Typed image

**The Jolly
Green Giant**
Brand logo
© The Pillsbury Co.
USA, c.1950
Lithograph

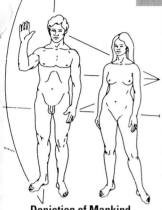

Depiction of Mankind
Detail from a plaque on the
spacecraft Pioneer 10; the first
depiction of the human form
carried to interstellar space
USA, 1972
Engraving on metal

**Dancing
Woman**
Detail
Roger Hilton
(1911–75)
England, 1963
Oil and charcoal
on canvas

The Human Form
© The Boeing Corp. USA, 1969
Computer-generated image

**Naked Girl
with Egg**
Detail
Lucien Freud
(b. 1922)
England, 1981
Oil on canvas

CONTRIBUTORS AND CONSULTANTS

Contributing artist

Valerie Wiffen's earliest memory is of drawing a picture on the sole of her kiddy shoe with a spent match. She is a graduate of the Painting School at the Royal College of Art, and holds the Diploma in Adult and Continuing Education from London University. Currently Program Manager for Art and Design at Hackney Community College, London, she also exhibits frequently at the Royal Academy, and regularly undertakes portrait commissions. She is a contributing artist to *Ways of Drawing Faces and Portraits* in this series.

Educational consultant

Carolynn Cooke gained a degree in Graphic Design from Canterbury College of Art and a Postgraduate Certificate of Education from Leicester University. She has been teaching art for over twenty years, and is currently Head of Art and Design at Impington Village College, near Cambridge, England.

SOURCES/BIBLIOGRAPHY

In addition to the original artwork shown in this book, many books, journals, printed sources, galleries, and collections have been consulted in the preparation of this work and of the Index of Possibilities. The author and editors would like to express their thanks to all artists who have contributed to the preparation of this volume. The following will make useful and pleasurable reading in connection with the history and development of the art of drawing the human figure:

Andy Warhol, K. Honnet, Benedikt Taschen, 1990
Art Deco, A. Duncan, Thames & Hudson, 1988
Asafo, P. Adler and N. Barnard, Thames & Hudson, 1992
The Atlas of Early Man, J. Hawkes, St. Martin's Press, 1976
Botticelli, G. Rouchés, Editions Brann, 1953
British Art since 1900, F. Spalding, Thames & Hudson, 1986
The Dada Movement, M. Dachy, Rizzoli, 1990
Drawing Today, T. Godfrey, Phaidon, 1990
Dufy, A. Werner, Thames & Hudson, 1987
The End of Expressionism, J. Weirstein, University of Chicago Press, 1990
Eric Gill: The Engravings, C. Skelton, Herbert Press, 1990
F. Léger, G. Néret, Cromwell Editions London, 1993
Fashion and Surrealism, R. Martin. Thames & Hudson, 1988
Giotto, P. Gay, Editions Brann, 1953
Henri Matisse, V. Essers, Benedikt Taschen, 1990
Image of the Body, M. Gill, Doubleday, 1989
Indian Painting, P. Rawson, Editions Tisné, 1961
Inner Visions: German Prints from the Age of Expressionism, Portland Art Museum, 1991
Japanese Graphic Art, L. Hajek, Gallery Press, 1976
Kroller-Müller Museum, Zonen Gratische Inrichting, 1977
Leonardo da Vinci, Yale University Press, 1989
Miró, R. Penrose, Thames & Hudson, 1970
The National Portrait Gallery Collection, NPG Publications, 1988
Opium: The Diary of a Cure J. Cocteau, Peter Owen, 1957
The Paintings of L. S. Lowry, M. Levy, Jupiter, 1978
Picasso: In His Words, H. Clark, Pavilion, 1993
Picasso's Picassos, D. Duncan, Macmillan, 1961
Raphaël, J. Mesnil, Editions Brann, 1951
Roger Hilton, South Bank Center, 1993
The Story of Cybernetics, M. Trask, Dutton, 1971
Toulouse-Lautrec, P. Hulsman and M. Dortu, Thames & Hudson, 1973
'Self-portrait,' *page 6, by kind permission of Helen Bishop*